From Here

Poems Inspired by Poetry

Monty Vern

Contents

About From Here

- 4 -

From Here is a collection of poems that have been inspired by poetry, the poetry of others as well as the poetry of my life.

The illustrations included in this collection explore 'found patterns', which like the poems, often led me to surprising and beautiful results.

About the Author

Monty Vern is an independent American author and illustrator. Monty grew up in the beautiful countryside of Vermont and currently lives and creates in Shanghai.

Previous titles include:

Apples Eating Zebras

Monty's Almanac 202X

Monty's Very Short Shorts

Thirteen Words (volume I, II, and II)

From Here

(from "Here" by Arthur Sze)

From here,

Is a story about a

Poet writing his words lingeringly, as a snail

Leaves a trail from its journey's beginning on

The narrow stem to the curled end of a

Glistening wet

Young leaf.

The first touch of green on a naked pine still with shivers

From the winter's cold winds and

Uncertain dreams

Of

A coming spring.

From here,

The poet coaxes a

Fresh line of thought, young and green

Capturing the curiosity of an artist's iris

Whose paints stood idle in

December.

From here,

By the

Moon's reflection in the topaz

Water's light

The artist captures images of

The

Star-speckled night's sky.

From here,

The poet and artist are one

When a stanza fizzles and stops.

He closes his eyes, hearing,

The silence and conjures a

Vision — a fig leaf on a twig

An offering of imagination to break

The quiet and

Discover a song that listens

To its own muse while waiting for

A bite by a fig-leaf nibbling deer.

From here,

The artist channels the

Art

Of

The

Ventriloquist.

From here,

The

Poet bows his head to a new obsession

Deciphering a strange dream of

A

Kleptomaniac

That was compelled to

Pilfer his words, to steal

Rhythms and rhymes and hide them in a red

Box next to forgotten pushpins.

From here,

The

Art

Of

The

Poet is lost with no alibi.

From here,

There is only one

Word to put in front of the other in walks

Of thoughts heading into

An

Abandoned

Story, to be resurrected as a farmhouse

Is raised by rough and worked hands and

A song is spun by one who hears

The tapping toes of a

Tarantula dancing a Tarantella.

From here,

Another one.

A story about a dreamer that dreamed

Of a

Star-batheing brown bear

Who caught the waxing moon with its claw

And

The moon's light died.

From here,

We return to the artist who mastered the art of a

Ventriloquist by calling the humpback

With the poet's voice and the whale

Leaped

Out

Of

The

Ocean.

From here,

The

Tale of the whale curves inward and outboard;

Turns fueled by a high-octane motor

Stopped

By sudden impact with shallow shoals but

Still turning awkwardly around a

Bent axle; as man

Limps forward despite all the chaos he's made

And he/she/they/it

Refuse to

Make sacrifices to save this

Island

Of life but rather row in downward spirals with

One

Oar.

From here,

The

Poet artist became actor,

Creating new worlds to forget

Their/her/his

Sadness and erase the smudged lines

Of sniffles and

Tears from when the world wept.

From here,

The

Art

Is our form of

Prayer.

From here,

Our lost marbles

Our pushed buttons

Our thumbed thimbles

Our tossed dice

Our stuck pins

Our smudged stamps

Our sweaty beads.

From here,

Alone, one

Becomes

None and I'm terrified.

From here,

One

Wanders, wonders, and wants

To

Believe in what he/she/they cannot see

As

A

God

Believes in humanity and sees

Some promise still and

Awaits our minds to become

Clear

Or turn to amber.

From here,

We are one.

The Poet is the Artist is the Ventriloquist is the beached

whale is

The cold and clear

Early spring air uplifting the season's first leaf on the naked

pine.

On This Day

- 15 -

The dog sleeps lazily at my feet, stretched out in the sun

streaming through a double-paned window.

Baba bends over a garden plant still bare from winter's

cold, his wrinkled hands working shears.

Mama sits slumped in front of a war playing out on TV; a

war from a generation ago, but not unlike today's. I guess.

My wife is several rooms away. Sounds like the kitchen; a

cabinet door opens and closes. A pot, I think, clanks.

I'm sitting on a wooden chair typing out these words;

listening to pop music that is too upbeat for my mood.

Across the world, my mom watches over her husband,

amongst equipment beeping signals of an uncertain future.

I imagine her strong, but I second-guess myself with worry.

This is when we usually speak each week. Sharing thoughts,
both poetic and banal.

Sometimes reminiscing of days long ago. More often just
connecting in the here and now.

These moments are when I pray for faith. When I wish
getting down on my knees had more meaning. When I'm
not ok with being powerless. When I don't feel the serenity
to accept things as they are. When all I can do is write
these words and pretend to pray.

Dancing to the Blues Upon the Morning's Light

For John and all those that love him

He did not hear the sun set.
Did not see the musical sounds of evening.
Or feel the moon's light upon his gently shut eyelids.
Or return the touch of love upon his heart.

Or so it would seem to an observer's eye.

Through the lens of love we witness
Him dancing to the blues upon the morning's light;
Lifting his face to feel the warmth of a new spring;
Fiercely protecting his loved ones in an eternal embrace;
And smiling while saying "Ho-hum"
To the wonder and beauty of the moment.

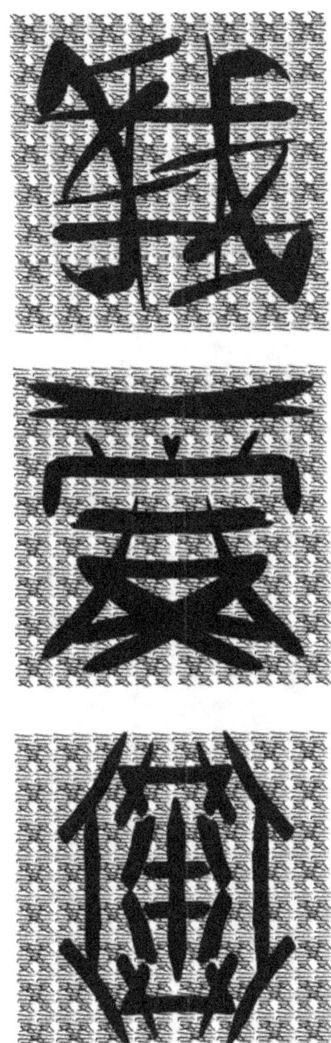

Rediscovering Sight

(from "After Apple Picking" by Robert Frost)

I

Chase the cannot

From the rub

Of darkness, embrace the

Strangeness

Of yes, peeling my eyes out from

Underneath my

Lids, rediscovering sight.

Sun-Bleached Blond

(from "The Tropics in New York" by Claude McKay)

Skin bronzed to a rich cocoa.

Hair sun-bleached blond, tied up in

Long braids hanging down past her ear pods

And

Shoulder straps, to the dancing twin alligator

Tattoos glistening beneath the dribbling juice of ripe pears.

Folly

- 24 -

Tilting at windmills

Avocado dreams

Foamy whips of froth

A needed tonic

Hurry, Hurry, Hush

(from "The Gong of Time by Carl Sandburg)

Rushing waters of our time;

Ebbing tide says

Hurry, hurry, hush.

Un-lived memories race by;

Yanked away by the

Quickening gong

Of

Our impatient time;

Shh! Will you

Pause a moment to live?

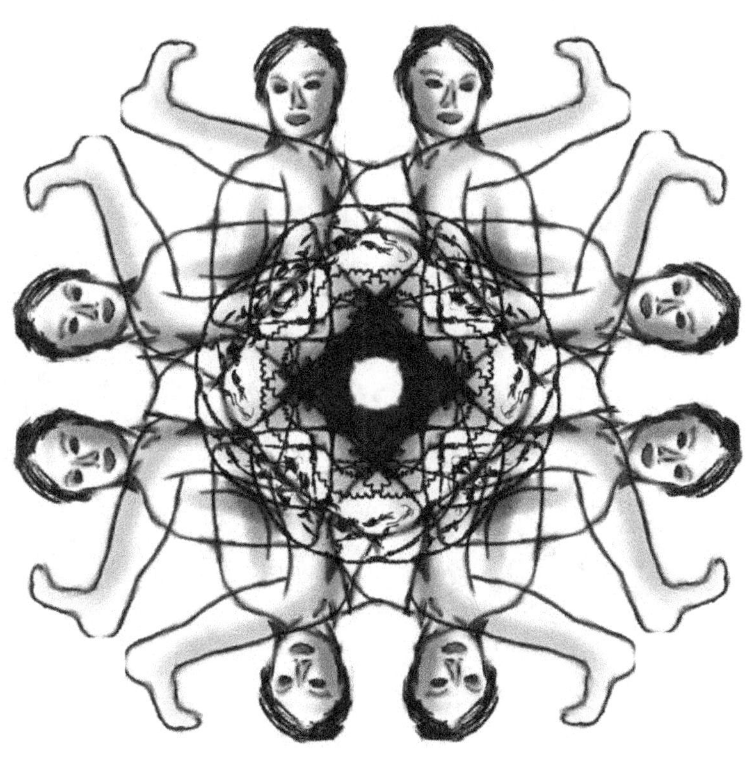

Reflections

(from "Laundry" by Ted Kooser)

She licks her upper lip, coating it with a

Slick layer of shine, highlighting the pink

Pigment of knock-off Tom Ford she stole from the main

house

Up the dirt road from her trailer.

She checks out her long legs in their scuffed

And

Red heels in the rusted

Sheet metal mirror on the wall, her sunken

Cheeks appearing elegant only in

Her mind, where flowers bloom from weeds.

She puts on

A pout, the

Kind of pout intended to catch the men on her line;

She imagined reeling in the cute one among the five

That sat on the liquor store steps under the single pale

Streetlight drinking Blue

Ribbon in their grease-stained workshirts

Rolled up

To

Their

Elbows.

She sucks in

Her mentholated tobacco breath, tasting raspberry

Sweetened naturally with sugar canes

Grown down south where belles like her belong in a

Home among good,

Clean,

Folk that watch over the crew

Of

Sugar cane cutters, or perhaps, raspberry pickers.

She puffs out

Her breasts, one nipple slipping out of her sagging dress, an

early

Blossom coaxed from its spring green sleeves

Glistening wet

With

Dew.

She reaches her bony arms up tall and

She near—

ly pushes them

Through the trailer roof to touch a

Thousand stars. Her dress rising above her sharp hips

exposing a pair

Of

Bright

Yellow

Panties

Urging

Them

On.

Green Shoots

(from "The Tropics in New York" by Claude McKay)

Green shoots and

Early buds bathed dewy

By spring dawns

And

Sunbeams mystical

With whispering mist above glistening blue

Puddles reflecting partly cloudy skies.

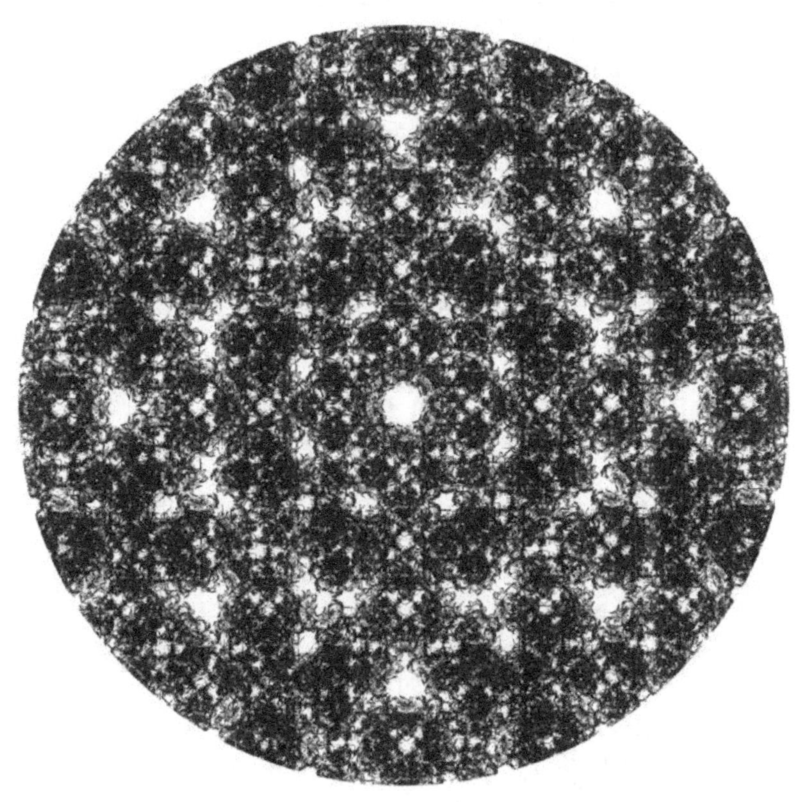

Little Brown Bird

A little brown bird perched upon my nose.

Talons scribing fresh wounds of all it knows.

A blue rat stands nearby at attention.

Reading each line and interpreting intention.

A orange cat plays with my eyeballs.

Pulling them to and fro from across the hall.

A patchy dog sleeps in the corner unaware.

Of all the troubles in this world to take care.

Horse bones hold together the chair.

I sit.

I wonder if this is the heavenly bit.

I start to feel its hooves trotting upon my seat.

Building to a gallop in a quickening beat.

Now sprinting into my belly and chest.

Showing my heart the wild wild west.

Lifting me to its muscled back so high.

I see beyond the old horizon in the sky.

He bends his neck, setting me down.

Before chasing the sun's next round.

I sit upon the earthly ground.

Grateful the world's turned once more around.

Gifting me the chance to see.

What this little brown bird has to say to me.

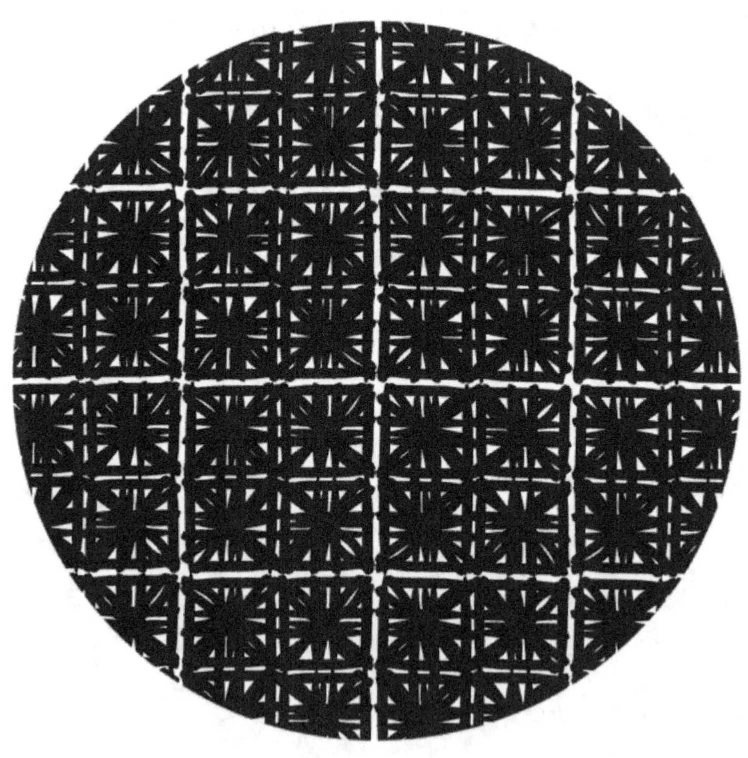

A Mid-Winter's New Moon

(from "Spring" by Mary Oliver)

Soft pillows stained wet by the

Anger streaming down her sun-setting sky

Flushed cheeks; She is,

No was, the warmth in my black and blue

Existence; I abandoned her or

No, I banished myself from the

Cool rain

That falls

On a stifling hot mid-August night with

Its

Splashing spills

Of

Encouragement coaxing me open to see the beauty of a

pearl.

From the blue-blood hue around

Exhausted eyes and their

Mourning wreath

Of

Darkness,

And the

Salt-soaked pillows, Her light leaves

And I shiver naked in the bitter cold of

A mid-winter's new moon; Let the

End of my time on this world

Unfurl.

Swimming with the Otters

(From 'Of Fathers of Daughters' by Hannah Aizenman)

How far can I fathom?

I'm into the deepest of waters.

Am I a keeper?

I'm swimming with the otters.

Am I a broken old fan?

I'd have been one of the draft dodgers.

Am I on your mind foremost?

I'm an imperfect scholar.

Am I a leaver?

I regret, yes, of mothers.

Am I a giver?

Of all five quarters.

Am I a failure?

I'm a victor of rathers.

Am I faithful?

I'm an imperfect supporter.

What about me do you gather?

I'm not there, but we're here, together.

Is it me you fear?

I am my disorder.

Am I a phantom?

I'm enough drama for the operas.

Am I a defender?

I cross borders.

Am I a frayer?

I cross wires.

Am I a good friend?

I'm prescribed by the good doctors.

Am I my own author?

I'm unsure of the gospels.

Am I grazing life's field?

While I'm waiting for slaughter.

This Night

(Inspired by Mary Oliver's "This Morning")

This night will end in mourning

The black and blue sky will bleed into red

The dark silence broken by willow's weeping and

Birds singing longingly for soul food.

This night will end and

I don't know how to begin again.

Where are the answers to be found

When even the moon has lost its way?

This night will be no more, no more,

I call out in prayer, as if I believe, to anyone

That will listen to my cries;

What else can I do?

This night will end and

Nobody has answered yet;

Have their eyes not opened?

Or is it my eyes that are closed?

This night will end with

The impatient sun taking the sky;

A thousand, million stars fading;

And I'm still without wings.

This night will end in morning

And despite not knowing how,

I will begin again; simple,

A miracle is taking place.

Out of My Mind

(From "In the Yellowstone" by Harriet Monroe)

Little,
Upon the head of a pin
Threatening to prick
Fast and furious geysers
Spitting
And
Sputtering.

Not at all little,
Sea-sized foaming
Geysers
That
Gurgle
Out
In tall-tales fabricated of
See-through sails pulling the
Mind's calyx
Of
Morning
To glory
In whirling pools.

Unbridled laughing

Geysers

That

Tickle my fancy and dance

In

The

Name of the spirits, our father, and the sun;

And

Spread

Folly upon their

Cast-off robes

Like

Down feathers escaping from lace

And wafting over

The

Techno-colored rocks.

Angry, raging

Geysers

That

Can't wait to rush

Out

From the reach of

Good intentions with scorching hell

Raised neurosis and with

A

Great

Strike of lightning and its grumpy rumble of noise

And

Blurt

Out

Curses across the vast

Sky, summoning the demonic dragon

With gulps

Of

Lusty urges and steam

And

Finishing

Upon her breast, sink

Back

Spent and wearily

Into

Singed darkness.

Gay and glad

Geysers

Escaping the forest like nymphs

Dreaming of

The

Mid-night sun

That

Arises

When sleep is slim

And

Nude

Figures cast shadows out

Of

The

Sweet, hot

Musky, dark,

Earth

And

Ebbs into a stand

Of trees

Poised

In

Twilight's beauty

Awaiting a

Moment

Perfect for un-veiling

Their

Wild brows

And

Boyish breasts

In

The cooling mist.

Clip-winged

Geysers

Broken spirits

Of

Smothered fire

That

Fail to rise,

Not tall,

And

Limp, not straight,

Like

A

Half-cooked noodle, a sequoia

Seedling stepped upon by heavy boot and

Aborted plume

Falls short of the

Sky

With

Tepid foam.

O,

Wild

Geysers, choral

Fountains

Of absurdities forever

Singing

To laugh-tracks and

Squelching the seething

Voices forever

Boiling

Disquiet in

Politics of despair from too deep

Places

To be safely conceived and

Leaping

Forth

For

Joyful and bright

Moments

Before disappearing into

The

Air.

How

Do

You

Like

It

Up

Here?

Why

Must

You

Go?

Going back?
Going to?
Will the
Spirits
Of
Light and darkness
Remain, or what?

Do

You

Tell

Them

Down

There

About

Your

Little

Adventure, your brief, glorious

Life

Out of my mind and in

The

Sun?

Pockets Full of Heavy Emptiness

Pockets full of heavy emptiness;
Large coins spill, plinking upon the porcelain;
After a quarter century still uncomfortable
Squatting above this foreign land.

Rooms occupied by missing faces;
Calls to dinner full of hollow bass;
Daily routines of other's comfort food,
And click-clacking complaints of rising prices.

Knotted-muscles pump thinning blood,
Watered-down by time and distance;
They told me to eat more red-bean porridge,
But I was raised on molasses and milk.

A weak tea leaf on the fifth pour,
Spent and floating just below the surface,
Sapped by the hot, humid, stifling air,
Dreaming of my temperate origins.
Viral infections, political and biological;

Empty, unpolluted skies, jets stand idle;

Sketched borders, once dotted-lines, solidify;

Am I on the wrong side?

The Illustrated Woman

My bold lines highlight the curve of her back
Bent under the sun.

My charcoal shading provides a cool shadow
For her to rest under.

My roughly sketched outline of her almond eyes form
wrinkles
As she smiles watching a drafted child quickly running by.

My accidental smudges hint at the years past and their
heavy memories.

Her hands are twisted knots, perhaps from age, but mostly
just from my lack of skill.

I play with color but settle on grey. She seems to agree.

Avocado Toast

(from "The Unnamable River" by Arthur Sze)

Feeding each other breakfast in bed, we lay in our smell;

Supple eggs on toast with buttery rich avocado

Sipping tea of steeped blossom

The blush of your naked cheeks true

A fading memory of passion

Reignited by the gentlest kiss

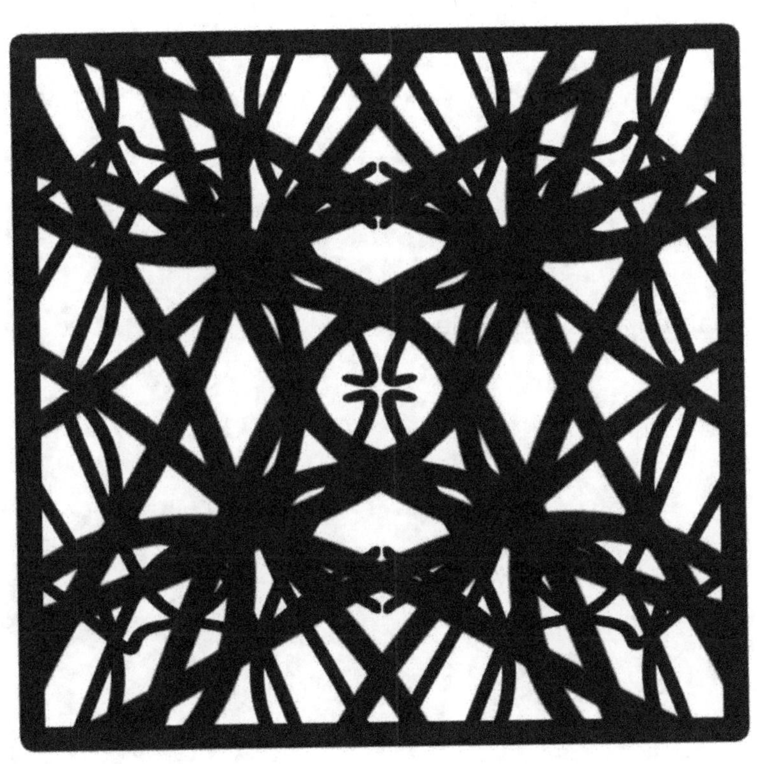

Ars Poetica

(Inspired by "Ars Poetica" by Archibald MacLeish)

A poem should not mean but be

I breathed a song into the air

With your breath

Shattered

I have no interest in being here
No interest in seeing your pain
Of being by your side as you call out for help
As your shattered bones burn fire

I wish I was anywhere else but here
Somewhere where I don't hear your cries
Where the lights aren't glaringly bright
And the air doesn't smell like disinfectant

I don't want to be here
To share you with nurses and doctors
To watch them care for you in ways I can't
To feel helpless to help you.

I wish to turn back time
To be the one driving, crashing, breaking
To be the one crying out for help
The one laying here shattered

I want to be the center of attention
The focus of all the nurses and doctors
The recipient of the morphine drips
And a rainbow cocktail of pills

I want you to be at my bedside
Whole and healthy
The strong, confident woman
That knows exactly what is needed

I've no interest in being here, but I am
I'm here to hold your hand and listen to your cries
I'm here to do the heavy lifting when needed
I'm here even though I'm helpless to help you

I wish to be anywhere but here, but my wish won't be
coming true
Selfishly I want to be the broken one, not you
But wishful thinking will not take away your pain
Nor will it help mend your shattered bones

So here I stay doing the best that I can do
Exactly where I belong, helplessly loving you

Unforgettable

He was beautiful in his own majestic way. Sad eyes with lashes that seemed to go on forever. Grey skin wrinkled after years of basking in the sun. Calloused, dusty feet from so many miles trekked.

She was beautiful in every conceivable way. Almond eyes with dark chocolate centers. Radiant skin, translucent in the filtered sunlight. Porcelain feet disappearing into elegant heels.

He stood silently, swaying, almost swinging with musicality. Looking into an unseen distance with somber longing.

She strode with confidence, hips swaying the air around her. Eyes smiling coyly below her hat brim, lips red and inviting.

He sunk onto his calloused joints, no more miles to trek, trapped behind bars as children and couples played beyond reach.

She turned her head toward him, shiny chestnut hair swaying long down her back. Gently pointing with her delicate hand, her voice practically sung, calling out to him.

Reflecting in his large sad eyes, the couple stood side-by-side. The girl looking his way. The boy seeming awkward and a bit shy as he looked down upon the melting ice cream he held.

Closing his wizened eyes, never forgetting his freedom times, he saw his past in their future, and gifted them with a blessing, for perhaps the last time.

Without so much as a word, just a smiling grin, the girl turned to the boy and proceeded to smush the ice cream he held all over him. The boy guffawed and practically snorted ice-cream up his nose, as his laughter released.

Knowingly and at peace, with the couple's laughter caressing his floppy ears, he let himself sink to a peaceful slumber.

Unknowingly blessed, the couple departed. A past stitching together their future as their first date at the Nagoya Zoo

etched into their memories.

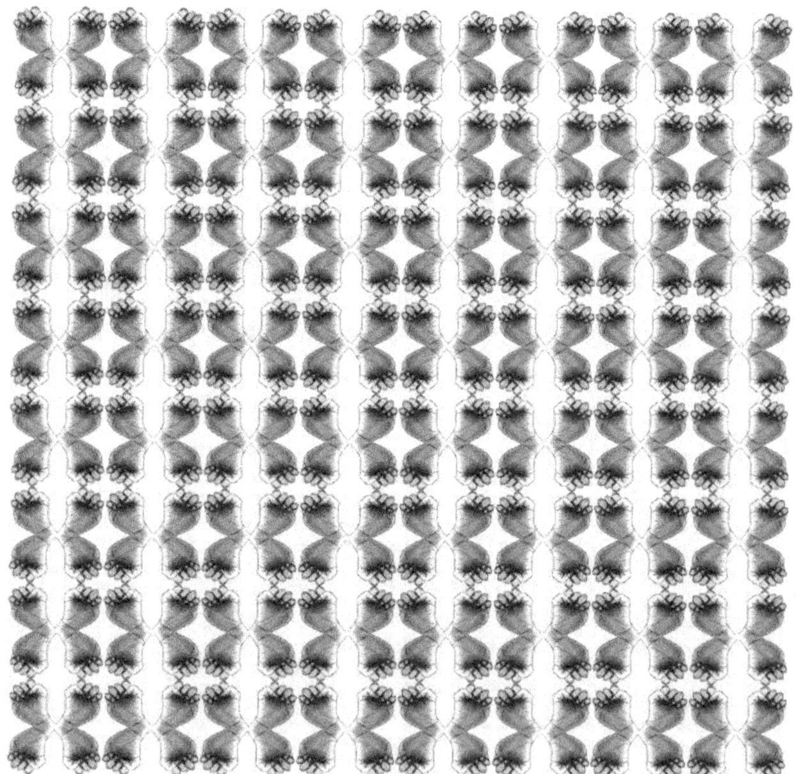

The Crescent Moon's Gentle Bend

- 71 -

The sky darkens as the day's warmth wanes

The moon's blue light flickers awake

And earth begins to shiver

Tall trees curving over

In the evening wind

Mimicking the

Crescent moon's

Gentle

Bend.

So Be It

They spoke foreign words.

About god, and church, and prayer.

Words, defined, but meaningless and empty to me.

They cursed, but in the name of Jesus.

Words I understood but not in this context.

They welcomed me to pray along.

They said it was ok to be an unbeliever.

That he would save me.

Would lift me up with light.

Know and love me anyway.

I sincerely doubted this.

But I prayed in the only way I knew how.

I said 'thank you'.

Not to him,

But to his followers that were reaching out.

They seemed broken, like me.

Loners in search of acceptance and human connection

Isn't it strange that only by searching for an improbable

higher power, we discover each other?

"Amen", they said.

Later, I looked it up and learned it means "so be it".

So be what? I wonder.

Perhaps I'll be back next week to find out.

Perhaps not.

"Re-Souled"

He spoke of a soft heart;

Of kindness and acceptance;

Supple from hard use,

Like a pair of well-worn boots;

More than once "re-souled".

His face familiar,

This man, a brother,

Yet I felt the stranger;

His words generous, loving, vulnerable;

Spoken, maybe, but I'd never heard.

A deeply calm rumble,

His sandy voice

Smoothed my sharp defenses,

Blunting points and dulling edges;

And yet, somehow, I felt safer.

Perhaps,

Now

I'm

Ready

To

Listen?

The Wanna-Believer

Today I pray for the first time,

As a wanna-believer,

For a taste of life's colorful palette;

To feel your love, your acceptance;

To accept that I'm worthy of your forgiveness.

Today I pray for the first time,

Maybe not with belief, but with want;

A wanting too deep to be filled alone;

Too wide to be crossed in this world;

So I seek a higher passage.

Today I pray for the first time,

Welcoming your presence;

Not needing to understand;

Eyes shut so that I might see;

Heart open so that I might feel.

Today I pray for the first time,

To accept that I cannot change without help;

For the courage to receive your hand,

And find peace through your wisdom;

Amen.

Notes

Many of the poems in this collection have been inspired by the poetry of others. In each case the source poem has been credited just below the title.

Poems credited as "from" are generally of the Golden Shovel form or slight variations on this form. The Golden Shovel form was created by the poet Terrance Hayes, whose poem "Golden Shovel" is based on Gwendolyn Brooks' "We Real Cool" which references the phrase "Golden Shovel". In the Golden Shovel form a line (or lines) are taken from an existing poem and a new poem is created using the words from the original line(s) as an end word in the new poem. So, if the form has been used strictly, one can read the source line(s) of poetry by reading the last word of each line in the new poem.

Poems credited by "inspired by" have, as the name implies, been inspired by the referenced poem but is not of the Golden Shovel form or its variations.

Poems that do not credit another poem are wholly original works inspired by the 'poetry of life'.